OFFER IT UP

OFFER IT UP

A STORY OF FAITH, ONE MAN'S

BATTLE WITH CANCER, AND A

WITNESS TO HOW GOD USES OUR

SUFFERING TO HELP OTHERS

JEFF KROHN

Information on Exodus 90 courtesy exodus90.com

 Exodus 90

Cover design by Jeff Krohn

RELIGION / Christian Living / Spiritual Growth
RELIGION / Christian Living / Inspirational

ISBN: 979-8-9922128-0-8

3 5 7 9 10 8 6 4 2

First edition

To my wife and kids who encouraged me, prayed for me, and did the things I could no longer do during this fight. Your support is a beautiful reflection of God's love.

To my best friend who stood by me as a prayer warrior, shoulder to lean on, and ear to bend.

To an indispensable friend who checked on me often and prayed unceasingly for me throughout this journey.

And to everyone else who prayed for me and encouraged me as I fought this battle.

Contents

PREFACE

Why write this book? In the fall of 2023, I wrote a "witness" for a men's retreat where I told a group of men the story of my cancer journey. I found that the twenty minutes I was given was not enough to share everything I wanted to.

Although it can be difficult to tell your personal story, I found myself excited to share. I realized that parts of my story are cautionary, exciting, encouraging, and faith-filled. I wanted people to hear it.

Even though I did not keep a formal journal during my cancer battle, I did keep quite a few notes. After several people expressed interest in hearing more about what I've been through, I realized that combining my witness with my notes could produce a short book.

It became both a cathartic exercise for me to reflect on my journey and a means to share my story and all of the lessons I have learned. I hope others find it encouraging and inspiring.

Throughout this book, I will mention many people. Although it sometimes makes the story a bit awkward to tell, I have intentionally excluded names to preserve the privacy of my friends, family, and acquaintances as much as possible. They have all played an important part in this adventure. I wish I could provide them with credit here, but their comments and actions are somewhat personal. I suspect that they may not want to be called out, even in a positive way.

At the end of each chapter, I have included reflection questions. These are based on what I learned or struggled with during that part of my journey. If you are reading this book alone, I encourage you to take a moment after you read a chapter to reflect on these. Or, better yet, pray with these questions. If you are reading this as part of a faith group or book study, these make great discussion questions.

My intent is not for this book to be primarily a story about me. If readers reflect and pray on the questions at the end of each chapter, and on the scripture passages, then use my story to change their relationships with God and one another because of it, I will have been successful.

> *Don't shine so that others can see you.*
> *Shine, so that through you, others can see*
> *Him.*
> C.S. Lewis

If you like to journal with your prayer and reflection, there is a companion hard cover *Reflection Journal* for this book. It presents a brief summary of each chapter, then provides the reflection questions from this book with ample space for journaling.

1

An Invitation

I was working from home on January 16, 2019. While I sat at my desk that morning, my wife texted. She was substitute teaching at the parish school that day and had heard that an acquaintance of mine, and a very active person in our parish church, had collapsed and died the night before. He was only 47 years old.

He was not a close friend, but I struggled to work that day as I kept thinking about the fragility of life. I thought about the last time I talked to him. I thought about the lunchtime workouts we occasionally did together at the gym. I thought about how the lives of his wife and five children would never be the same.

He was an extremely faith-filled person, so I was not fearful for his soul. But that doesn't mean death is easy. After all, even Jesus wept at the death of his friend Lazarus.

Jesus wept.

John 11:35

A few hours later, a friend of mine texted. We knew one another from the men's Bible study we both attended—and the drinks we would have together with the guys around his basement bar after many of our Bible studies. He and his family were new to the parish, and he was actively trying to get involved and meet people. He was reaching out that morning to invite me to join him and some other men in a spiritual exercise called Exodus 90.

It was perfect timing that day to say yes to the invitation. After hearing about the death of someone so young, I was reflecting on how death can hit any of us at any time and how I needed to get more serious about my own faith.

While I used to be on fire for the faith, my spiritual life had diminished to barely more than attending Sunday Mass. I knew I needed new motivation in my faith life. I also wanted to get to know him better and develop a closer friendship, so without really knowing what Exodus 90 was, I enthusiastically said yes.

I would soon learn that Exodus 90 is an intense ninety day spiritual exercise for men. It is ninety days of fasting twice per week, no snacks, no alcohol, no sweets, no desserts, no television, no unnecessary phone use, no unnecessary computer use, cold showers, a workout three times per week, a commitment to an hour of prayer daily, a daily check in with a fellow participant (known as an "anchor") to encourage one another through the difficult exercise, and weekly meetings with the entire "fraternity" of nine men who were participating.

It was as hard as it sounded, especially the cold showers! But after ninety days, my life was changed forever.

I learned to pray better than I ever knew how to before. I learned that I could do hard things and deny myself worldly pleasures if I set my mind to it, had faith, and had people around me to encourage me. I developed friendships with the other eight guys in our Exodus 90 fraternity.

And the friend who invited me to do Exodus 90 and with whom I wanted to develop a closer friendship? By the end of the 90 days, we became best friends.

There are friends who pretend to be friends, but there is a friend who sticks closer than a brother.

Proverbs 18:24

Little did I know how important all of those things would be just a couple of years later. God was giving me a strengthened faith, and friendships, that would soon help me weather some serious trials.

Reflection Questions

1. Have there been any significant moments in your life when you were called to renew or deepen your faith? Was there a particular person or group that inspired you to start taking your faith more seriously?

2. How does the awareness of life's fragility affect the way you live your daily life and prioritize your spiritual and personal growth? What changes can you make today to live with more purpose and awareness?

3. Have you ever reflected on the reality of your own death (*memento mori*)? Are you prepared for it spiritually and practically? Have you told your loved ones, both family and friends, what they mean to you before it is too late? If not, why not?

2

THE JOURNEY BEGINS

I admit it. I'm not the model of health. Exodus 90 notwithstanding, except for an occasional game of racquetball or an occasional trip to the gym, I have never exercised much. I like food and adult beverages, and my weight shows it. But then again, that's not too different from your average 48-year-old man. I may not be the model of health, but I am not too far from average either.

In September of 2021, I went to my doctor for a physical. Because of the Covid lockdowns I had missed my two previous annual physicals, so it was long overdue. Everything looked reasonably good, and the doctor was generally happy with my health. I got my usual admonishment to exercise more and lose weight, and the doctor left the room.

He immediately popped his head back into the room and said, "We don't normally do a PSA test on men under fifty, but do you want to add one to your lab work? We can use the blood we already have drawn."

I'm an engineer, so I thought more data is always better and quickly agreed to it.

The PSA, or prostate-specific antigen, level is used to screen for prostate cancer. Many other conditions can cause suspiciously high PSA levels as well, and the absolute number does not necessarily mean anything. A high number warrants investigation, though, and as an increasing trend over time can indicate the possibility of prostate cancer.

I don't know what motivated my doctor to decide to run a PSA test when it isn't standard for someone my age, but I would soon be grateful for whatever combination of medical intuition and divine intervention was involved. Without it, I would not be here today.

I didn't think about it again until the next morning when my doctor's nurse called. She told me that my PSA was 8.2 and my doctor wanted to follow up on it. He referred me to a urologist.

My primary care doctor has always been quick to refer me to a specialist with even the slightest hint of needing a specialist's opinion. Sometimes it sends us on the proverbial wild goose chase, but I generally prefer to be extra cautious with medical issues. My ears did perk up when the nurse said my doctor wanted me to take the urologist's first available appointment.

Two weeks later, I found myself in his office. I immediately liked his bedside manner. He was friendly and took time to answer questions. I tend to bother doctors with detailed technical questions. Unlike most doctors, he seemed excited to talk about the details and to teach me what was happening. I felt like I had a medical partner, and a highly qualified one at that, despite his young age. He's the type of person I could easily enjoy a drink with if he weren't my doctor.

In researching his qualifications, I discovered he had only just completed his residency. Yet, I had complete confidence in him. I think he also appreciated having me as a patient. Partly because I took an interest in my own health and he could have a higher-level technical conversation with me, but also because my case was unusual. I think he liked the challenge. I joked with him about how he had better at least get a research paper published after working on my case.

He ordered another PSA test, and we got a similar result to the one in my primary care doctor's office. Reiterating that absolute numbers do not mean as much as trends, but that absolute numbers this high are cause for concern, my urologist recommended having an MRI to see what, if anything, was going on.

A week later I went in for the MRI, and a few days after that found myself back in the doctor's office to get the results.

Even at this point, I did not think too much of all of this. It seemed pretty routine. In my mind, we were simply covering our bases and ruling out anything serious. So, when he told me that the MRI indicated that I had cancer, it didn't sink in right away.

My doctor explained that the MRI showed a cancerous area with a Gleason score of 7.

The Gleason scoring system indicates the aggressiveness and prognosis of prostate cancer. A score of five and below indicates that the cells are not cancerous, with scores of six and above indicating more aggressive cancer.

Although the Gleason score from the MRI indicated a moderately aggressive cancer, my doctor said he was not concerned. Often, prostate cancer can simply be monitored for years and never become a problem.

He did, however, want to do a biopsy to see exactly what the cancer looked like.

I couldn't believe it. Not only did I have cancer, I was 48 years old and I had what I considered to be an old man's disease. Men my age don't get prostate cancer.

I was pissed.

Not trusting.

Not hopeful.

Pissed.

> *Even youths shall faint and be weary, and*
> *young men shall fall exhausted; but they*
> *who wait for the Lord shall renew their*
> *strength.*
>
> Isaiah 40:30-31

I got home from the appointment and told my wife the news. Her mother passed away from cancer when my wife was only fourteen years old. Cancer is something that worries her. Having lost her mother as a teenager, she has a depth of understanding and a fear of cancer that I can never fully grasp.

We told the kids but were careful not to scare them with the "C" word. As adults we can process the fact that cancer does not need to be a death sentence. Kids, though, hear that word and immediately think the worst. The kids seemed to take the news in stride, like we had hoped.

Otherwise, I told no one else except my very closest friends and swore them to secrecy. I may have wanted to keep this diagnosis quiet, but I believe that close friends have a right to know major news in life—and to know it before anyone else except family.

A few days later, my best friend emailed with a question about something. I replied that I didn't have time to look into it because I was distracted by the cancer news.

He responded, "A little cancer got you worried? You got this."

I'm not proud of my reply. "Worried? Yes, I'm ******* worried."

I texted him and apologized. He was trying to encourage me, not minimize what I was experiencing. But in my stress, I snapped at him. He graciously accepted my apology and asked if he was still sworn to secrecy.

I told him he was.

I was not ready to admit what was happening. I was embarrassed to be 48 years old and have what I perceived to be an old man's disease.

I remember his response—"I think you should ask the guys to pray for you. If prayers work, and you and I both know they do, it seems to me that you could use a heap of them. I'm sworn to silence until you tell me otherwise."

Then he texted me this passage:

And which of you by being anxious can add one cubit to his span of life? Therefore do not be anxious about tomorrow, for tomorrow will be anxious for itself. Let the day's own trouble be sufficient for the day.

Matthew 6:27,34

Reflection Questions

1. When has a routine event turned into a pivotal moment in your life? How do you see God's hand in these moments?

2. How can vulnerability and openness within a supportive community of friends and family help us navigate life's trials?

3. How do you see the connection between your spiritual life and your physical well-being? How might a deepened faith provide strength during times of physical or emotional hardship?

3

WRESTLING WITH TRUST

A couple of weeks after I learned I had cancer, I went in for the biopsy to determine how bad it was. I grappled with the whole concept of having not just cancer, but a cancer that primarily strikes much older men.

As I was lying in the hospital bed waiting to be taken to the procedure room, my surgeon stopped by to check in with me. We talked for a while, then he said, "See you back there soon." before he walked out of the room. I had to laugh when I overheard him ask the nurse how to get to the operating room. It reminded me that he was new to the practice and barely out of his residency. Nevertheless, I had complete confidence in him.

The biopsy was surprisingly quick and nearly painless. I was home by mid-morning. As I sat at home recovering, a friend texted asking me what time the biopsy was. He wanted to pray for me during it. A little late, but knowing he was concerned and that he put in the effort to remember I was having the procedure that day meant a lot to me. Most of all, I value his eagerness to pray for me.

I continued to struggle with accepting what was happening, and even as a faithful person I struggled to trust God. The idea of having cancer so young bothered me a lot. I didn't understand why God would allow this to happen to me.

True believing means looking the whole of reality in the face, unafraid and with an open heart.
Pope Benedict XVI

One night on my way home from work, the Holy Spirit made me realize I needed to stop in the adoration chapel at church and work it out with Him. After all, *Israel* means "to wrestle with God". I needed to have a wrestling match with Him.

I knelt down on the floor in front of Jesus in the tabernacle, cleared my mind, and started praying for trust in God and His plan for me.

A few minutes later someone started practicing the organ in the church. I love the sound of the organ at Mass, but I was fuming. I was already in a bad mood, and now the music would distract me from my prayer.

Then, as I prayed for trust, I recognized the words to the song that was being played.

"Glory and praise to our God, who alone gives light to our days. Many are the blessings he bears to those who TRUST in His ways."

I had my answer.

Now that song has become inspirational for me, and much to the chagrin of the people in the pews around me, I belt it out whenever it is sung at Mass.

I will bless the Lord at all times; his praise shall continually be in my mouth. My soul makes its boast in the Lord; let the afflicted hear and be glad. O magnify the Lord with me, and let us exalt his name together!
Psalm 34:1-3

This was just the first of many times when I would pray during my cancer journey and get an amazingly clear answer from God.

Yes, sometimes He chooses not to give an answer in that moment. But I always get closer to God when I spend time with Him. Time with our Lord is never wasted. If we take the time to sit with Him and quietly listen, even when He doesn't give us answers He will give us peace.

> *Trust in the Lord with all your heart, and*
> *do not rely on your own insight. In all*
> *your ways acknowledge him, and he will*
> *make straight your paths.*
> Proverbs 3:5-6

It can be hard to submit to God's will. Sometimes it takes having no choice to force us there.

From this point forward my entire attitude about having cancer changed. I finally started coming to terms with the diagnosis.

I released my friends from their promise of secrecy and began asking my wider network of friends and acquaintances for prayers.

The next week, my surgeon called with the pathology results. The biopsy showed that it was indeed cancer, but it was not as serious as the MRI indicated. It was a Gleason 6, which is barely considered to be cancer. Based on its location, it almost certainly could not have spread.

We could just do "active surveillance". Active surveillance consists of a PSA test several times per year and a biopsy every year or two to check that the cancer is not growing further and to catch it early if it does. An inconvenience for sure, but not a big deal.

My doctor believed it could be ten years or more before we would need to do anything.

Because of her experience with her mom's cancer, my wife did not like the idea of active surveillance. She wanted the cancer gone. I understood but thought that if it was stable like the doctor thought that it was, I did not want to jump to major surgery and all of the side effects any sooner than I needed to. I did, however, agree to opt for surgery if there were ever signs of the cancer growing.

As word got out about my diagnosis, I received a phone call from a doctor I know at church. We had a nice conversation, and I came away with some recommendations and validation that the plan was a sound one.

I was starting to get in a better place emotionally. The cancer was stable. Life could go on.

The relatively good news about my cancer lasted less than a year. Just long enough for me to learn to trust God better.

God had a plan.

Reflection Questions

1. Have you ever experienced a time when trusting God was difficult due to life's challenges? How did you work through your doubts?

2. How has God shown you answers in unexpected ways? Are you open to seeing His hand in your life?

3. When you pray, do you take the time to listen to God's response? Most people do not literally hear a voice when they say God spoke to them. In what ways do you experience His voice?

4

A Friend's Suffering

The summer after my cancer diagnosis, in July of 2022, my best friend's eighteen-month-old son had a choking accident and was rushed to the hospital.

I was at a business lunch when I heard about it. I cut lunch short and immediately reached out to see what they needed. He asked me to stop by their house to get some things for them. Soon, I joined him and his wife at the hospital with their son.

Later that night after their out-of-town family arrived, I decided they probably preferred it to be family at that point. I left the hospital and went to my car to head home for the night.

While we were all praying for a miracle, I also knew deep down that without a miracle this was not likely to turn out well. I held it together in front of everyone that day, but as soon as I got into my car, I couldn't hold it together any longer. I sat in my car and bawled like a baby.

It must have been fifteen minutes before I pulled myself together enough to drive home.

I couldn't shake the memory of the look on my friend's face and the pain in his eyes in that hospital room with his son. I remember it to this day.

I kept replaying over and over in my mind when his three-year-old son ran up to me in the hospital waiting room, looked up, and asked me when his brother was going to wake up.

I had to do *something*.

I was struggling again to trust God. How could He let this happen?

As I prayed on the drive home from the hospital, I begged God to save him.

Then, I asked God to let me take on some of the pain I saw in my friend's eyes in that hospital room with his son and take it away from him.

I prayed that God would let me help carry some of my friend's cross for him.

God put on my heart to offer up my cancer as redemptive suffering for him. It wasn't much—after all, the cancer didn't seem too serious—but it was *something* I could do to help him get through this. It was the least I could do. It's what best friends do for each other.

> *Now I rejoice in my sufferings for your*
> *sake.*
> Colossians 1:24

Two days later, his son passed away.

For readers not familiar with redemptive suffering, in Catholic theology redemptive suffering is the belief that human suffering, when willingly united with the suffering of Christ, can have a redemptive or salvific value.

Suffering is not meaningless or pointless, but can be a means of participating in Christ's own passion, death, and resurrection. Through suffering, individuals can grow in holiness, offer something back to God, and contribute to the salvation of others.

Catholics believe that when a person suffers—whether from illness, loss, hardship, or injustice—they can offer their suffering to God, uniting it spiritually with the suffering of Christ.

This act of "offering it up" allows them to find purpose in their pain and to be spiritually united with Jesus, who suffered for the salvation of all.

The Bible speaks of this idea in passages such as this one from St. Paul:

> *Now I rejoice in my sufferings for your sake, and in my flesh I complete what is lacking in Christ's afflictions for the sake of his body, that is, the church.*
>
> Colossians 1:24

This verse does not suggest that Christ's suffering was insufficient, but rather that Christians are invited to share in His suffering, bringing spiritual benefit to the world.

Through suffering, a person can participate in Christ's mission. We are united with Christ's suffering for the salvation of the world. Suffering can be an act of intercession for the needs of others.

While redemptive suffering acknowledges the reality of pain and hardship, it is ultimately grounded in hope when it is embraced with faith—the hope of eternal life with God.

The resurrection of Christ assures us that suffering is not the final word; it will be transformed by God. Suffering, in this sense, becomes a way of participating in the life, death, and resurrection of Christ, leading to ultimate healing and salvation.

Reflection Questions

1. Have you ever experienced a time when you were able to find meaning or purpose in your suffering? How can you deepen your understanding of suffering as a way to participate in God's plan or offer support to others?

2. Would you be willing to offer your suffering for someone you love? What about for an acquaintance? What about for a stranger?

3. In what ways have you been inspired by others who are facing challenges, and how does that shape your approach to your own struggles?

5

AN UNEXPECTED CROSS

A week after offering up my cancer as redemptive suffering for my friend, I had a routine checkup with my doctor. After having my blood drawn, I sat in the room and waited.

These appointments are usually quite fast. The lab does not take long to test the blood, then the doctor comes in to give me the results. I am always in and out in fifteen or twenty minutes. This time I was waiting a lot longer.

Eventually, he walked in with the test results. He did not seem to be in his usual happy mood. There weren't the usual pleasantries. I had barely stood up from my chair when he—still staring at the piece of paper with my PSA result—said, "This result is interesting."

Then, he looked me in the eyes. "Your PSA is 16.8. It's doubled in six months. We need to operate."

I was in shock.

This was not supposed to become a problem for years.

I was never supposed to have cancer to begin with. Especially not at 49 years old.

I can't have life-altering surgery.

Bad things don't happen to me.

I quickly realized that no matter what was supposed to happen, no matter whether I wanted this or not, I had no choice.

Was God trying to teach me another lesson about trusting Him?

After I got in my car to drive home from the appointment I texted my wife. Was texting her the right way to inform her that major cancer surgery was necessary? Probably not. She had been concerned about this cancer from the beginning, though, so she was more relieved than upset. She saw the opportunity to finally have the cancer out of my body.

That night, we told the kids what was happening. Our approach with them from the beginning was to be truthful, but positive. They do not need to know all the worries or the negative possibilities. To understand that I had cancer, but that the doctor was going to remove it, was enough. We were careful not to scare them.

This diagnosis was harder on my family than I realized. Because my wife lost her mother to cancer at a very young age, she is particularly sensitive to cancer diagnoses.

It was incredibly difficult for me to hear from some other parents that one of my kids had run out of the classroom in tears during a class unit on cancer. I had no idea this was affecting them like this.

After giving the news to my family, I called my closest friends and asked them to spread the word. I needed prayers.

We have all heard the quote about how God will not give you more than you can handle. That sounds nice, but it's not true. He *will* allow us to have more than we can handle. But He also gives us the faith, grace, strength, and community to bear the cross. What we can't do is handle it on our own.

I thought about the timing.

I realized that it couldn't be a coincidence that things took a turn for the worse immediately after I offered up my cancer for my friend.

After all, I did ask for a cross to bear for him. God was answering my prayer. I joke that I was thinking more along the lines of mild inconvenience, though.

> *If I find my purpose in the morning, I'm*
> *content to give up my life in the afternoon.*
> Ancient Asian saying

When I was first diagnosed with cancer, I was too embarrassed to tell anyone except my family and my closest friends. Now it was bad enough that I realized I needed to spread the news and ask for prayers.

The parish community came through once again. I ended up on prayer chains not just at my parish, but throughout the world. My typically arrogant self was humbled.

At the time I offered up my cancer, I did not intend to tell anyone about offering it up. I was going to offer it up quietly as scripture tells us to do with our prayers.

> *But when you pray, go into your room and*
> *shut the door and pray to your Father who*
> *is in secret; and your Father who sees in*
> *secret will reward you.*
> Matthew 6:6

But it didn't take long to see God's hand in this. I had to share the story so that others could see it too.

God's timing is perfect. I hated that my cancer required surgery, but I was awestruck at seeing His plan begin to play out.

I may have started out too embarrassed to share my diagnosis, but now I wanted everyone to hear about how God is working through me.

> *And he went away, proclaiming*
> *throughout the whole city how much Jesus*
> *had done for him.*
> Luke 8:39

A week later I went in for an updated MRI to validate the decision to do surgery. Without another

MRI I would be undergoing major surgery based only on the results of a single blood test. As expected, the MRI confirmed that the cancer was growing quickly.

My prostatectomy was scheduled for September 15, 2022.

Knowing that after surgery there would be a long recovery ahead, my wife and I scheduled a short weekend trip. We wanted some time together to reflect on what was happening. We spent the weekend talking about life and about the kids. Most of all, we simply enjoyed being with one another. As parents of four kids, having one-on-one time is a luxury.

I arranged for time off work and began getting some things done around the house since I would be restricted from heavy lifting for several weeks after surgery. And I made sure things were in order for my wife, just in case.

There was one more thing to do before surgery. I had to be prepared spiritually.

As I was leaving a meeting at church, I ran into one of our associate priests. I told him about my situation and asked him if the sacrament of Anointing of the

Sick would be appropriate before surgery. He said it was, and with an excited tone of voice asked if he could be the one to anoint me. I consider him to be a friend, and I appreciate that he cared enough to want to be the one to administer the sacrament.

On Sunday, September 11, 2022, I was anointed. In four days I would be going in for surgery.

Reflection Questions

1. What cross are you currently carrying, and how can you invite God to walk alongside you?

2. What does friendship look like? What do close friends do for each other?

3. How do you recognize or interpret signs of God's hand in your life? How might sharing your experiences impact others?

6

UNDER THE KNIFE

F rom the beginning, I have wanted all the details I could get. I want to understand it all. I quickly discovered that most of the information I was finding online was either terribly outdated or plain wrong. Luckily, my surgeon was willing to humor me and provide me with all of the information I wanted.

I had watched videos online of this type of surgery. The precision of the robotic procedure fascinated me. I even asked my surgeon if he could record my surgery. He agreed, but unfortunately he discovered on the day of the surgery that the hospital's robot did not have that capability.

My surgeon was young, but I had total faith in him. I wasn't nervous at all about it. It was what had to be done. Although it is a major surgery, and a delicate one at that, it is fairly routine.

On September 15, 2022, we drove to the hospital.

I went through all of the pre-surgical preparation. I joked with the anesthesiologist that he had two jobs that day—to make sure I didn't die and to make sure that I didn't remember.

Then I sat there in the hospital bed waiting and praying with my wife at my bedside.

Shortly before the scheduled surgery time, my surgeon came in to tell me that the operating room was running late, so in turn my surgery would be starting late. I joked with him that I hoped he would be done in time to have a drink with his friends after work. He jokingly assured me, "Don't worry. I'll stay until we're done."

As I lay down on the operating table, I renewed my commitment to offering up my cancer suffering for my friend. I said a quick prayer and was soon completely under anesthesia.

It was planned to be a two hour surgery. Awakening from anesthesia, I did not have a sense of time. The recovery room nurse asked if my wife was in the waiting room. I said she may be picking up kids from school, but otherwise, she would be there. He laughed and said it was almost 8:00 pm. That's when he informed me that there had been complications. It had turned into a nearly five hour surgery.

I bet my surgeon needed a drink after that. I am glad he stayed until the end, too!

My wife sat patiently in the waiting room while the surgery took almost three times longer than expected. She is a smart woman who is highly knowledgeable about medicine. She knew something was going wrong. That was not easy for her, but her resilience is one of the things I love about her. She can get through anything.

The medical staff kept her well-informed and the waiting room staff even briefed her on where to find everything before they left for the night! I don't know how many rosaries she said for me while she waited, but I am sure it was many.

I soon learned that the cancer had started to grow into a different area than expected, which made it more difficult to remove than the surgeon anticipated. He was also being meticulous in an attempt to prevent the delicate surgery from causing damage to surrounding tissue. This is one of the major risks of this surgery. Damage to surrounding tissue causes lifelong side effects, and some amount of damage is inevitable even with a skilled surgeon.

During the process, a surgery that is usually almost blood free turned into a surgery where I lost two units of blood. The good news was that the cancer appeared to be confined and was completely removed.

My surgeon also removed seventeen nearby lymph nodes to check for cancer. The pathology would later show that there were no signs of the cancer spreading to any of these lymph nodes. Great news! It was highly unlikely to have spread if it was not found here.

Although the surgery was difficult, my doctor believed it was successful. After a couple of days in the hospital and a few months of healing, life should go on.

I was in the hospital for two nights. Although I was having surprisingly little pain, it was a major surgery that warranted observation. I spent my time catching up on some reading and praying. Not to mention watching every episode of *House Hunters* on HGTV. Twice.

It was only two days, but spending those days lying in a hospital bed made it feel like forever.

I must admit I was disappointed that there were no visitors other than my wife during my hospital stay. But it soon became clear how much support I really had.

Two weeks at home with nothing to do and a five pound lifting restriction was tough. I don't watch a lot of television or movies. So, like my time in the hospital, I spent a lot of time reading and praying.

My best friend and his wife took a trip to Italy the week of my surgery. They wanted to get away for a while after the death of their son. I could tell he was disappointed that he couldn't be in town to support me that week, and he even apologized for it. But they needed that time together, and I soon realized that I needed the prayers he would be offering for me in the Eternal City.

As they toured Rome, the texts started rolling in. He took a picture at each church they toured and in front of each relic they saw, then sent it to me with a note about how he prayed for me there.

As I was sitting at home recovering, another very close friend came over to visit. I was feeling down about the long road ahead, so his visit meant a lot to me. While we were chatting, my phone rang. It was a FaceTime call from Rome.

We all had a nice conversation, and as I hung up the call, I felt the presence of God that day in those friendships. Despite what I was going through, I am blessed. Not only do I have a supportive wife and wonderful kids, but I am also blessed with amazing friends.

Therefore encourage one another and
build each other up, just as you are doing.
1 Thessalonians 5:11

Reflection Questions

1. In what ways can we feel God's presence through relationships? How might your faith be strengthened by the support of others in difficult times?

2. How does the concept of offering our struggles for the benefit of others impact your perspective on suffering? What are other ways you might transform hardships into acts of faith?

3. How can reflecting on your blessings reshape your mindset in challenging times?

7

FROM HOPE TO UNCERTAINTY

My recovery went quite well. I was tired, but there was not the pain you would expect after major surgery. More than anything, I was bored.

I am not the type who can sit around for weeks. I always need to be accomplishing something. My wife took care of me and made sure I didn't overdo it.

The surgeon gave me a lifting restriction of five pounds for six weeks after surgery, so there was very little I could do. I couldn't even lift a gallon of milk. As far as I know, I only violated that restriction once— when our small dog got out while I was home alone. I had to chase him down and carry him back home.

I was off work for the two weeks following surgery, then I worked from home for another two weeks before returning to the office.

When the surgeon told me I would need a total of a month at home I doubted him. In hindsight, I wish I had taken more time to heal. Even though I was healing well, a major surgery like that wears a person out and there is little that can be done to help the healing process except resting.

Going back to work helped me get back into a routine, and other than dealing with some side effects from the surgery, life was beginning to feel close to normal again.

There were many follow-up appointments after the surgery, and with each one a new PSA was run to be sure it was decreasing. PSA is made only by prostate cells, so after a prostatectomy, the PSA should decrease to zero over about six to eight weeks.

I was encouraged to see that the number was decreasing just as it should.

Even though I had been spending a lot of time in doctor's offices because of my cancer surgery, I had to take care of my routine health. So, when it came time for my annual physical I went to the appointment like normal.

Although my surgeon was the one monitoring it at my appointments with him, I was excited to see my PSA level continue to decrease. So, while I was having my blood drawn for my physical, I asked the phlebotomist if she could add a PSA test to the blood she was drawing. She checked with the doctor, who quickly agreed.

Like most medical practices today, the results were online as soon as they were available, so I logged in and looked. It showed that my PSA had not decreased since the last test two weeks earlier.

I was frustrated by that but thought little of it. I assumed it was because I had impatiently asked for another test before they normally would have tested again.

The next day I got a call from my surgeon who had been sent the results by my primary care doctor's office.

My surgeon is one who is not afraid to call his patients himself and have long discussions. He tells things like they are. His bluntness combined with his friendliness is one of the reasons I like him.

This call was no different. He didn't sugarcoat anything. After the usual niceties to start our conversation, he said, "I saw your latest lab results. I'm worried."

I would put those two words among those you do not want to hear from your doctor.

"I'm worried."

Count it all joy, my brethren, when you meet various trials, for you know that the testing of your faith produces steadfastness. And let steadfastness have its full effect, that you may be perfect and complete, lacking in nothing.
James 1:2–4

He went on to explain that my PSA level should not have stopped decreasing. It was possible, and even likely, that cancer remained somewhere.

He told me about a recent technological development that can look for cancer metastasis—the PSMA PET scan. He wanted me to have the scan to see where there might be signs of cancer, or hopefully to determine that there is not any.

The surgery was supposed to take care of everything. How can there still be cancer? I was dumbfounded.

I reasoned that since none of the seventeen lymph nodes he took out during the surgery had signs of cancer there was no way any cancer could remain. That was the point of removing and testing them.

This had to simply be because I asked for another PSA test earlier than usual.

I would prefer that I wasn't the subject of this much medical intervention, but modern medical technology fascinates me.

A PSMA PET scan (prostate-specific membrane antigen positron emission tomography) sounds like something from science fiction. Although the technology is cutting-edge, the concept is simple.

Because cancer cells grow faster than normal cells—that's what makes them cancerous—they also metabolize glucose faster than normal cells. So, if a person is injected with radioactive glucose, the cancer cells will absorb more of the radioactive isotope than the normal cells will.

The PET scan can see where in the body the higher concentrations of the radioactive isotopes are. From there the doctors can infer where cancer is present.

Two weeks after the call where my surgeon said he was worried, my wife and I drove to the hospital for the scan.

I was injected with the radioactive glucose solution and was told to wait quietly for an hour in a chair in a darkened room while my cells metabolized the glucose. Then, I lay on a table that moved me through the PET scan detector. Quick and easy.

Driving home from the scan, we stopped for gas. While I waited for the tank to fill, I pulled out my phone and checked email. There was already an email from the hospital stating that the test results were posted to my online account.

I couldn't believe the radiologist had read the scan that quickly. But that was great! I was anxious to finally see that it was all OK and that life could go on.

That had to be the result, right? Bad things don't happen to me.

I logged into my account, opened the file, and started reading the report.

Even though I'm no doctor, it was not hard to understand the phrase "metastatic nodal disease".

As I scanned through the report, the reality started to sink in that the cancer had spread into my lymph nodes.

My heart sank.

This was bad.

This *could* be *really* bad.

The gas pump clicked off and startled me out of my racing thoughts. I got back in the car, looked over at my wife...and decided I couldn't tell her yet. I didn't know how I would tell her, and it certainly did not seem appropriate to tell her in the car. How do you tell your wife you have metastatic cancer?

But when Jesus heard it he said, "This illness is not unto death; it is for the glory of God, so that the Son of God may be glorified by means of it.

John 11:4

Shortly after we got home, I mustered the courage to deliver the news. We had a battle on our hands, and I couldn't fight it without her by my side.

Reflection Questions

1. How do you typically respond when faced with difficult or unexpected challenges?

2. What role does your faith play in helping you navigate times of uncertainty? How can you draw closer to God during these times?

3. How might you create a "spiritual toolkit" to help you navigate times of difficulty and uncertainty?

8

Into Battle

Although I had already seen the results, my surgeon did not know that and called the next day to give me the news. He recommended a medical oncologist at one of the top cancer centers in the area. I certainly did not know any, so I was especially grateful that I had full faith in my surgeon's judgment.

He also recommended that I consult a radiation oncologist that he knew. Healthcare in our city is world-class. We have many options to choose from. I was determined to assemble one of the most qualified teams of doctors in the area.

Anyone who has been through something like this, or some sudden tragedy, understands that time stops. You drop everything and focus on the crisis at hand. Plans are canceled and time with friends is postponed. You focus inward on yourself and your family.

Over the next few weeks, my life was consumed with medical appointments.

It was Christmastime. I was planning, as I always do, to take the last two weeks of the year off work. I enjoy being able to completely disconnect from work and relax with my family, surrounded by all the exciting anticipation of Advent and the joys of Christmas. This time to be with family and friends is precious when the rest of the year is so busy.

Instead, on December 12, 2022, my wife and I were meeting with my medical oncologist for the first time. I was blessed to have my wife with me at these appointments. She would advocate for me, and her knowledge and experience have made it so much easier to interpret everything the doctors said.

We immediately liked the oncologist and developed full confidence in his abilities. He has a reputation for treating cancer aggressively. There was no doubt that was what I needed.

Around 300,000 new cases of prostate cancer are diagnosed each year, and around 35,000 men die from it annually. It is the second leading cause of cancer death in men.

He explained again that prostate cancer at my age is unusual, and my cancer was showing signs of being particularly aggressive.

Fewer than 1% of cases strike a man under the age of 50. When it does, it's nearly always deadly. In younger men, it tends to be more aggressive than average prostate cancer. Combined with the fact that doctors are not screening for this cancer in younger men, it leads to a high mortality rate. By the grace of God, mine was caught early.

For thou didst gird me with strength for
the battle.
Psalm 18:39

The doctor explained that in most cases of metastasized prostate cancer, the treatment is two years of androgen deprivation therapy (ADT). Prostate cancer cells feed off of testosterone, so for two years they remove *all* testosterone from the body to attempt to starve the cancer cells.

This is where being young is the problem. Androgen deprivation therapy does not cure the cancer. It kills many of the cancer cells but only weakens others. For an older man, something else will kill them before the weakened cancer cells start growing again.

In a younger man like me, that would not be sufficient. I am likely to live long enough to see the cancer recur if we use ADT without other therapies too. My oncologist recommended we also use chemotherapy.

He wanted to fight aggressive cancer with aggressive treatment.

We agreed that that was the approach we wanted to use, and I wanted to start as soon as possible.

I'm the type who confronts problems head on. I am not afraid of the truth. I asked my oncologist what my chances were. He said it was tough to put numbers to an unusual case like mine. I pressed him for a number.

Finally, he told me I probably had about an 85% chance of survival.

My engineering mind started trying to put that into perspective. An 85% chance of survival sounds pretty good. But that also means a 15% chance of not making it. A 15% chance of succumbing to cancer sounds pretty bad. Put another way, a one in six chance of this cancer killing me.

It's funny how thinking about something in reverse can totally change the perspective on it.

I also realized that Russian roulette has the same odds. And who would be foolish enough to play that game?

I consider that the sufferings of this present time are not worth comparing with the glory that is to be revealed to us.
Romans 8:18

The plan was to immediately start a hormone-blocking drug (bicalutamide), then as soon as it could be arranged to start a hormone-blocking shot (leuprolide) and six chemotherapy treatments (docetaxel).

At the end of chemotherapy, we would add another hormone-blocking pill (aberaterone). The total treatment time would be two years.

I picked up the bicalutamide prescription that night on our way home. I was ready to attack this as hard as I could and do it now.

When we got home, I logged into the patient portal and read my doctor's treatment plan. It was mostly standard stuff and a summary of our earlier conversation.

Then, I read words that stopped me in my tracks.

"The goal of treatment is to prolong life."

No mention of a cure. To *prolong* life.

What does that mean? How long is "prolong"?

The reality of this was starting to sink in.

As I would talk with people about my cancer, I would often get some dismissive version of, "My dad had that too." It was frustrating that no one understood that mine was diagnosed younger, was more aggressive, and had metastasized. Mine wasn't your grandpa's standard prostate cancer.

One of the biggest mistakes we make in life is thinking we have more time. It is easy to believe it can never happen to you.

But it can.

Ask me about it. Ask my best friend about it. Ask so many other people to whom something *has* happened.

That evening a friend texted asking how the appointment with the oncologist went. I had found a cartoon earlier that week that I thought was apropos to my situation, so I responded with it. It shows the Grim Reaper coming for a man, but the man refuses to go with him.

With everything I was facing and the harsh treatment I was about to undertake, there were many emotions that I wrestled with. One emotion I never had, though, was fear.

Confused. Frustrated. Upset. Lonely. Angry.

But *never* fearful.

Faith conquers fear. This was one of the first moments I realized that the faith I've claimed to have and have been trying to live out is real. My trust was in God, and I had no fear.

Faith doesn't always take you out of the problem. Faith takes you through the problem.

Faith doesn't always take away the pain. Faith gives you the ability to handle the pain.

Faith doesn't always take you out of the storm. Faith calms you in the midst of the storm.

Anonymous

Throughout all of this, my wife's faith has been exemplary. She prays for me constantly. Nearly every morning I can find her sitting downstairs with her coffee and her rosary enjoying some time with God before everyone wakes up.

Reflection Questions

1. Do you believe that bad things can't happen to you? Or are you the opposite and think that only bad things happen to you? Where do you think the right balance is?

2. How does your faith in the resurrection of Jesus shape the way you view your life and your future, especially when facing the reality of death? How can this eternal perspective influence how you live today?

3. How can you see God's hand in the people and circumstances that come into your life, especially in times when you feel most vulnerable or uncertain?

9

THE FIRST DOSE

I was surprised by how much preparation goes into starting cancer treatments. First up was a bone density scan. The hormone-blocking therapy depletes calcium, so we need a baseline of bone density before we start treatment. This also means I needed to start a daily calcium supplement.

Chemotherapy is serious enough business that I contacted my priest for a second anointing.

Then, the following week was an "education" session at the cancer center to make sure I understood what I was about to undergo. Seriously? It seemed silly to need to be educated on all the side effects and risks of treatment. What choice did I have? Can we get started already?

Nonetheless, it was informative to understand and be prepared for the side effects that I was about to experience. It turns out they are easier to cope with on paper than in real life.

I left the appointment even more determined to fight.

That night I got a text from a friend of mine. He invited my wife and I, and a few other couples, over for a pre-chemotherapy get-together. I think he knew something I didn't yet. I was going to need a lot of support, and this would cheer me up and get me started with a good attitude as I began treatment.

Unfortunately, my wife was not feeling well. She stayed home while I attended. It felt odd without her by my side that evening. Even so, it was a great time with great friends celebrating Christmas and the beginning of chemotherapy over some drinks, food, and friendship.

A cheerful heart is a good medicine.
Proverbs 17:22

The next day, December 20th, 2022, my wife and I went to the cancer center for my first treatment.

There was a kind of strange anticipation and excitement I had starting all of these treatments and beginning the process of beating this cancer.

I'm the type to go head down and deal with a situation when I hit adversity. This was no different.

We walked into a large, bright, open room with dozens of recliners. Whoever designed the treatment room at the cancer center put a lot of effort into attempting to make it a comfortable environment.

I chose a recliner and sat down while my wife pulled up a chair beside me. As we waited for the nurse to come over, I looked around the room. Nearly everyone was obviously very sick. Most lacked hair, many looked gaunt, and some were skin and bones.

Was this my fate too?

Even in their condition, there were a number of joyful people. I knew I was going to be one of them.

The nurse came over, and after some small talk she inserted an IV. Then, she started several pre-medications to help counteract the side effects of chemotherapy.

About twenty minutes later, the premedication was complete. The nurse returned with an IV bag of the chemotherapy drug.

I couldn't help but laugh at the irony of the nurse putting on a paper gown to protect herself from the chemicals she was about to inject into my veins.

As the chemotherapy started flowing into my body, I could taste it.

This chemotherapy drug can cause permanent loss of feeling in the fingers and toes if blood flow to the hands and feet is not restricted while it is administered. The nurse returned to place ice packs on my hands and feet to slow down the blood flow.

We sat there, talking and taking it all in. It was surreal to be sitting there. An IV in my arm. Ice packs on my hands and feet. Less than six months earlier I had a minor cancer diagnosis. Now I was undergoing chemotherapy for stage 4 cancer.

It was never far from my mind, though, that I was still offering up my cancer suffering for my best friend. I was happily taking on some of his suffering through my own. His son had passed away not even six months ago.

I don't think he was ever comfortable with what I was doing. But it was clear to me that it was part of God's plan. And, regardless, it was my gift to give.

Was this helping him bear his cross? How could I know? I leave that up to God. What I do know is that our suffering is never wasted if it is willingly united to Christ's.

Ninety minutes later, we were done. The nurse removed the IV, I received my leuprolide shot, and we were on our way.

The worst part of the experience was the ice packs on my hands and feet for an hour.

While I was excited to start treatment, it would not take long for me to realize that this would not be easy.

That afternoon, my best friend texted. He was having some of the guys over for drinks that night. I was feeling fine, despite having just started chemotherapy, so I accepted the invitation. I always enjoy time with friends. It was especially important to me now that I was beginning treatment. I needed that support.

We sat around his kitchen table sharing stories and laughs. Inevitably, the conversation turned to my cancer.

It's normal for men to rib each other. There is a saying that "True friends give you a hard time to your face and say nice things behind your back". I hope they say nice things behind my back. They certainly gave me a hard time to my face that night.

And I loved every minute of it.

I can find the humor in any situation. Even irreverent gallows humor can be a terrific way to lighten a mood. Along with prayer and the support of so many people, what could be better than humor from close friends to keep my attitude up and help me get through this?

> *Where joylessness reigns, where humor dies, the spirit of Jesus Christ is assuredly absent.*
>
> Pope Benedict XVI

By the time the night ended, they had asked if they could use some of the life insurance money to throw an epic party.

I agreed.

Then they asked if they could have me at the party *Weekend at Bernie's* style.

I insisted they do.

One of the embarrassing side effects from the surgery is incontinence, so they decided to start a diaper drive for me.

The ADT treatments take away testosterone. So, they kept referring to my "transition" and discussed what my new pronouns would be.

Brutal.

You get the idea.

Awfully harsh.

> *Faithful are the wounds of a friend;*
> *profuse are the kisses of an enemy.*
> Proverbs 27:6

One of the guys came up to me later and apologized. He said he was uncomfortable with it but didn't know how to stop the other guys.

We all laughed so hard that night. Yes, it was harsh. Yes, they went way too far. But honestly, I appreciated it. Only good friends would do that. It was meant in fun, and it certainly lightened my mood.

I went home that night grateful for those friends and the time we were able to spend together. And excited that the first chemotherapy treatment was done. Five more to go.

Reflection Questions

1. What is your reaction when you need to start something difficult? Do you dread it? Do you avoid it? Do you attack it head on?

2. When you face a challenge, do you bring it to God in prayer? Do you ask for His help? Do you get mad at Him?

3. Can laughter, even in the face of suffering, be a form of trust in God's ability to bring light into the darkness?

10

CHEMO, COVID, AND CROSSES

The day after my first chemotherapy treatment, I was not feeling well. It had all the markings of Covid. When Covid went through our house over a year earlier I was bedridden for two weeks and my wife spent a week in the ICU. Since then, we haven't worried much about Covid. We knew we had immunity and that the virus was weaker now than at the height of the pandemic.

But I was in the middle of cancer treatment. I was one of those "immunocompromised" people now. I took a Covid test to confirm my suspicion, then called my doctor. He prescribed an antiviral medication, and I rested for a couple of days. No harm done. But it was a good reminder that I needed to be careful now. Things were different. This is serious stuff.

After recovering from Covid, the side effects of chemo started to hit. My fingers were feeling slightly numb. My stomach was queasy. I took my anti-nausea medication for the first time. It would become one of my go-to drugs during chemotherapy.

I sat down for dinner and salted my food. After a few bites, I decided I needed more salt. Not enough. I added some more. Still bland. My wife is an amazing cook. I assure you she does not make bland food. I don't know how much salt I ended up putting on my dinner that night before I realized the chemotherapy had caused me to lose my sense of taste for salt.

It was another sign of the seriousness of what was happening.

I spent the next several days in a down mood. But it also felt selfish to be down about this cancer compared to the crosses other people carry. Everyone has their own things in life to deal with. I am not unique in that regard.

I thought about others who have it worse. I haven't experienced the loss of a spouse or a child. I haven't experienced a divorce. I haven't experienced most of the bad things many others have. I'll likely survive, at least for a few more years.

Other people with cancer won't. A fellow parishioner at church, not even ten years older than me, passed away from cancer while I battled mine.

So did the brother of a friend of one of my kids.

Another friend's teenage daughter was diagnosed with cancer. She will live, but not before undergoing miserable treatments including the amputation of her leg. The permanent effects I am facing from my cancer are nothing compared to that.

Through prayer and some sound advice from others, I've come to realize we can't compare our crosses. We each have our unique ones. But we *can* help one another carry them.

> *God is our refuge and strength, a very present help in trouble.*
> Psalm 46:1

My second chemotherapy treatment was scheduled for January 10, 2023. My wife could not accompany me this time, so I was planning to go alone. Luckily, none of the chemotherapy side effects kept me from being able to drive.

I was at work finishing up some things before I left for the cancer center and got a text from my best friend.

"Send me the details for chemo. I want to heckle the nurse before she sticks you with poison."

Yes, we can help one another carry our crosses.

When the cares of my heart are many, thy consolations cheer my soul.
Psalm 94:19

What a friend who would remember when my chemo treatment was. What a friend who would be willing to sit there with me to keep me company and help get my mind off what I was going through. What a friend who would do it on his son's birthday. He left the cemetery after visiting his son and came straight to the cancer center.

I was humbled.

After meeting with my doctor, I took a seat in the treatment area. Shortly after the nurse started my IV, he came walking in and pulled up a chair. I felt incredibly blessed. We spent ninety minutes joking around, and of course, giving the nurse a hard time.

As he left, he said, "I guess now it's my turn to pray for you."

We must have made an impression. The nurse called me the next day with some blood test results and said, "You guys sure had fun yesterday!"

I don't know if she meant that positively or as a criticism that we had disturbed the other patients!

He kept me company at another treatment too. At nearly every appointment he was not at, the staff would ask where my "fun friend" was.

Bear one another's burdens, and so fulfil
the law of Christ.
Galatians 6:2

Reflection Questions

1. How does the presence of suffering in your life make you more aware of the suffering of others? How does your faith shape the way you view and endure suffering?

2. How do you accept help or encouragement from others when facing trials? How might this deepen your relationships?

3. What practical steps can you take to strengthen your spiritual and emotional resilience in times of trial?

11

Joy in the Journey

At the recommendation of my oncologist, I decided to have genetic testing done to determine if my genetics were a contributing factor to getting cancer. The results came back with mixed news. The testing revealed that I have a HOXB13 mutation, which is associated with up to a twenty times higher risk of developing prostate cancer than the average man.

The good news is that it was not a BRCA mutation. The HOXB13 mutation is associated with prostate cancer, while the BRCA mutation is also associated with breast cancer.

So, my boys are likely to be at higher risk for prostate cancer as they get older. With this information, they will know they need to get checked early. Fortunately, I cannot have passed on a gene that will put my girls at higher risk for breast cancer.

I settled into the chemotherapy routine. Every three weeks I visited the cancer center for another treatment. And every day the side effects were getting worse. Eventually, I would lose all sense of taste.

Sitting at my desk at work on one particularly stressful day, I was running my hand through my hair while reading a proposal. I looked down and saw a handful of hair.

The doctor had said I might see some thinning of my hair. This seemed to be a lot worse than "some thinning". Within a few weeks, it would be nearly gone.

Before each treatment, I would meet with my doctor for what they call a "toxicity check". Initially, I thought this meant a check to see how well the cancer was responding to the chemotherapy—how toxic the drugs are to the cancer.

But, no, it means a check to see how well *my body* was responding to the chemotherapy. They needed to check that I was tolerating it and that my body could safely handle another treatment. Yet another sign that this was serious stuff.

Despite the gravity of the situation and the side effects of treatment, I kept a joyful attitude about it all. I was determined to beat the cancer and was still in a phase of excitement about attacking it.

For this slight momentary affliction is preparing for us an eternal weight of glory beyond all comparison, because we look not to the things that are seen but to the things that are unseen; for the things that are seen are transient, but the things that are unseen are eternal.

2 Corinthians 4:17-18

Each time I sat down in a chair in the treatment area and looked around, I could see people who looked like they were suffering more than me.

But then I wondered—if I am sitting among them, I must be in as bad of shape as they are. Maybe the only thing that made it seem like I was set apart from them was my attitude.

I wondered how many of them had faith. Without a doubt, it was my faith that was keeping me going. It is amazing what hardships Christian joy can carry a person through.

Even though there seemed to be a lot of silent suffering in that room, there was a lot of community too. There was a lady with breast cancer, barely older than me, who was there at the same time as I was for most of the treatments. She sat there with a friend when her husband couldn't be there. They laughed and undoubtedly were having a fun time, even in those circumstances. Frequently, they would bring cookies to share with everyone.

After a total of six chemotherapy sessions, that phase of my cancer treatment was done. It felt great to be done and to move on, but it also felt odd. There really is a sense of community in that treatment room. To be done and not see those people every three weeks was a strange feeling. Sometimes I wonder how their stories ended.

The week before my final chemotherapy treatment, my wife had made plans for us to go out to dinner with some close friends of ours. My 50th birthday was the following week, so we wanted to celebrate. Finishing chemo was an excellent birthday gift, too!

I cleaned up from an oil change I was helping another friend with, then we left for the restaurant. We walked in and headed toward the back of the restaurant where our friends said they had a table.

As I turned the corner, a room full of people started singing.

It was surreal. Did fifty or sixty people really go out of their way to celebrate my birthday with me? My wife had thoughtfully arranged, with the help of a close friend of mine, to throw a surprise party for me.

We mostly celebrated my birthday, but in my mind we were also celebrating the end of my chemotherapy, the joy of living another day, and those friendships that had developed over the years.

I thank my God in all my remembrance of

you.

Philippians 1:3

All night we laughed and shared stories—each of which got funnier the more we drank. It was probably a good thing our parish priest had left the party early in the evening!

The following day I looked at pictures from the night before. How blessed I am to have a wife and close friends who would go through the effort of arranging that. How blessed I am to have that many friends who would show up to celebrate with my wife and me.

I needed that.

I also noticed in the pictures that I had almost no hair.

Although chemo was over, I decided that I would look better if I shaved my head rather than have just a few strands of hair. It would be months before my hair started to grow again. Except for my eyebrows. They never came back. I'm not sure what's up with that. It's funny how without eyebrows my face has a constant look of surprise now!

With my gratitude from the party in mind, I realized that it had been a while since I last updated "the guys" on my progress. I sent this text:

Brothers,

I have not updated many of you for a while.

As divine providence would have it, shortly after offering up my cancer as redemptive suffering I learned that surgery did not cure it and the cancer had spread. God wanted me to offer up more.

Aggressive prostate cancer almost never hits someone at my age. When it does, the outcome is rarely good. So the doctors threw the book at this.

I had my last chemo treatment today! I start radiation this fall. I'll continue androgen deprivation therapy until December of 2024. Still a long road ahead, but the treatments are working!

The doctors gave me an 85% chance, so I'm counting on Jesus' words to Mary and Martha in the gospel a couple of weeks ago—"This illness is not to end in death, but is for the glory of God."

I'm learning a lot during this. Most of all, I have an amazing group of friends and brothers surrounding me. I never would have predicted the support and prayers I've received from all of you.

So, THANK YOU.

Whether you're praying for me, checking in on me, joking around with me, visited after surgery, wrote me a heartfelt note, or kept me company during my chemo treatments, I'm grateful. Many of you have your own battles, yet chose to join me in mine.

God bless you all. Please continue to keep me in your prayers as I fight this. And know that I'm praying for you too.

Shortly after sending the text, one of them responded with words that rang true and mean a lot to me to this day:

> You are well loved and prayed for at
> almost every meeting I go to at church. We
> put this in HIS hands and whatever is HIS
> will. HIS plan is always better than our
> plan. You continue to live your life in a
> way that is an inspiration to the rest of us.
> We can't know the future. That's probably
> a good thing for we would only mess it up
> if we did. So, we live in the present. Know
> that we all love you but the one who really
> matters loves you more. Peace, Brother.

Reflection Questions

1. It's been said that we make time for the people who are important to us no matter how busy we are. How well do you live this with both your family and your friends?

2. How can joy and gratitude transform your experience of life's challenges?

3. How do you share joy with others even in times of personal struggle?

12

A LONELY FIGHT

I had always heard that having cancer is lonely. I never understood that until I had it myself. Even with so much support, you are fighting this battle that few people understand. A battle that's never far from your mind. A battle that consumes your life. A battle that constantly reminds you that you're fighting it. A battle where you know you need to lean on God. Even then, He can feel pretty distant.

But other people bring Him closer. My wife and kids have been amazingly supportive. They pray for me often and ask others to pray. They willingly answer the inevitable questions they get about how I am doing. More than anyone, they have been constant reminders that I am not alone in this.

And my friends have been there for me. One checks on me often, prays for me, and offers more help than I can even accept. I know he'd be there for me no matter what.

Others have written heartfelt notes that mean a lot to me and leave no doubt in my insecure mind what our friendship means to them. What a gift.

I'll never be the same again. I try. I put on a good face on the challenging days. But the reality is I'll never be able to do everything I used to do. I will live the rest of my life with the life-altering consequences of the treatments.

Despite that, on most days I'm joyful and faith-filled. It's funny how you don't fear death when you have faith. What I fear more than anything is leaving behind my wife and kids.

Even without fear, there were plenty of nights where I laid in bed, sometimes with tears in my eyes, and realized that even though the treatments seemed to be working, the fact is I have aggressive stage 4 cancer that's been worse than expected at almost every turn.

I lay there selfishly hoping and even praying that the cancer would kill me because I was tired of dealing with the treatments, side effects, and emotions.

He asked that he might die, saying, "It is enough; now, O Lord, take away my life; for I am no better than my fathers." And he lay down and slept under a broom tree; and behold, an angel touched him, and said to him, "Arise and eat." And he looked, and behold, there was at his head a cake baked on hot stones and a jar of water. And he ate and drank, and lay down again. And the angel of the Lord came again a second time, and touched him, and said, "Arise and eat, else the journey will be too great for you." And he arose, and ate and drank, and went in the strength of that food forty days and forty nights.
1 Kings 19:4-8

I thought about the fifty pounds I've gained because of these treatments. The reality hits that this is not a cancer that usually gets cured. It is likely to return in the future and we do this all over again. And hope it works again.

I thought about that feeling at Mass when I look at the altar and picture lying in a casket in front of that very altar someday, maybe sooner than I hope.

I thought about the day when my doctor calls and tells me the cancer is back. Where will I be? How will I tell my wife, kids, and friends?

But through the grace of God, in the morning I wake up beside a beautiful wife and I see four amazing kids. Almost every day I get a call or text from friends. There may be challenges, but life is good.

> *More than that, we rejoice in our*
> *sufferings, knowing that suffering*
> *produces endurance, and endurance*
> *produces character, and character*
> *produces hope, and hope does not*
> *disappoint us, because God's love has*
> *been poured into our hearts through the*
> *Holy Spirit who has been given to us.*
> Romans 5:3–5

While I was undergoing chemotherapy, I had people tell me after Sunday Mass how they were praying for me. Some even came up and introduced themselves with "You don't know me, but I wanted you to know I heard what you're going through and I'm praying for you."

Wow. I guess it's tough to hide a cancer battle when you've lost your hair.

The number of people praying for me is overwhelming, although there was one example where prayer did not go as expected.

After a meeting at church, one of the people who was there whom I didn't know approached me. Like so many others, he had heard about me but didn't know me. He asked me to tell him my story, so we sat in the church for a while chatting.

During our conversation, he revealed that he has a charism for healing. He said that he would keep me in his prayers, but he did not want to pray for healing for me despite his charism.

I was taken aback until he explained that after hearing how I had offered up my cancer as redemptive suffering, he felt my suffering was helping my friend too much for him to want to pray for my healing.

> *Is any among you sick? Let him call for the elders of the church, and let them pray over him, anointing him with oil in the name of the Lord; and the prayer of faith will save the sick man, and the Lord will raise him up.*
>
> James 5:14-16

There were numerous times people offered prayers for me. At every Knights of Columbus meeting since my diagnosis, someone asks the men there to pray for me. Prayers work. But it also is a great feeling knowing that the person who asked people to pray for me that night was thinking enough of me to speak up.

At one meeting someone even suggested that the entire group of men pray over me. I think most Catholics would find it uncomfortable to kneel in the middle of the room surrounded by forty people laying hands on them and praying. It certainly feels more like an evangelical Protestant approach. But just because in modern times we don't usually pray for others this way does not mean that we shouldn't learn from our evangelical brothers.

I felt those prayers that night.

I would soon realize that people who I did not remember telling about my cancer were asking me how I was, and mentioning that they had prayed for me at this meeting or that meeting at church.

It took me a while, but I eventually realized that one of my friends who is highly involved and attends many different bible studies and meetings at church was ensuring that everyone knew about my battle and that everyone was praying. What an amazing prayer warrior!

And they came, bringing to him a paralytic carried by four men. And when they could not get near him because of the crowd, they removed the roof above him; and when they had made an opening, they let down the pallet on which the paralytic lay. And when Jesus saw their faith, he said to the paralytic, "My son, your sins are forgiven. I say to you, rise, take up your pallet and go home."

Mark 2:3-5,11

In the account of Jesus healing the paralytic, we see that he is healed, not only by his own faith, but because of the faith of his friends. Your circle matters.

Through my own trials and those of my friends, I have learned that God often communicates his love for us through other people. I have seen Christian community in action.

But to reap those benefits, we must first sow.

Allow me to propose some questions.

How involved are you in activities with other people? How well do people know you?

It's been said that we become the average of our closest friends. When you look at the people you spend the most time with, are they challenging you to be a better person? A better spouse? A better parent? A better friend? A better child of God?

Do you associate with people who have your back?

Do you text your friends often to check on them? Do you call your friends just to chat? Do you invite them to hang out and spend time together?

Yes, we're all busy. But God created us as a social people.

The whole world needs to hear two things
with strength and power: "God loves
you", and "I love you". You must say it
often to your friends. This world is not
starving from lack of money. It's starving
from a want of love.
Mother Angelica

Build those relationships now, before you need one another. Because eventually you will.

Reflection Questions

1. In what ways have you seen God's presence through the support of others during difficult times?

2. What role does prayer play in your journey through suffering? How do you discern God's answers, especially when they are not what you expect?

3. What roles do friendships and community play in your life? How do you nurture those relationships?

13

AN UNINTENDED WITNESS

M any people have encouraged me throughout this struggle. Often, they say some version of the same thing. That I'm projecting Christian joy throughout this. That I'm setting an example. That I'm making an impact. That I'm an inspiration.

I didn't pay attention to it initially other than to sincerely appreciate the kind words. But over time, as more and more people said these things, it became a pattern. I began to realize they were not merely kind words. It was true. People were seeing in me something I never saw in myself.

I never realized how much others were watching me. We were on a break at our annual men's retreat when someone whom I only knew by name approached me. He looked at my name tag to confirm it was me, shook my hand, introduced himself, and told me that he had heard about me and that he needed to meet me. He proceeded to tell me how he had been praying for me.

Later that night, another guy approached me in a similar fashion. He said that he had been watching me each Sunday at church. He noticed after my cancer surgery how I struggled to kneel and to get up and down. He said he saw me lose my hair. Between what he had heard about me and what he saw by watching me every Sunday, I had inspired him with my example.

Apparently, I was becoming a celebrity of sorts because of my cancer.

I'm not sure I am comfortable with that. I feel so unworthy of this kind of praise. How can someone as flawed as me be inspiring to anyone?

One friend has texted me often during this journey to tell me he is praying for me, and he usually ends the text by thanking me for being an example of faith and an inspiration to him. Really? Me?

The culmination of these comments happened when I was talking with a relatively new friend. We had been acquaintances for quite some time. He knew what I was going through, but we hadn't been close enough to talk about it in detail until more recently.

The conversation started with talking about exercise and health, then soon turned to my cancer. My friend stopped and said, "If I say what I want to say I'm going to tear up."

We sat in silence for a couple of minutes while he composed himself. I was anticipating what this could be that needed to be said. What could choke up someone like that?

Then he said, "I hope if I ever have to go through what you are going through that I could handle it as well as you."

Wow.

I appreciate everything people have said to me throughout this. But these words in particular hit home and meant—and still mean—a lot to me. Someone I did not know that well through much of my cancer battle was impacted by my example. I'll remember and be forever grateful for that interaction.

Along with offering up suffering, God can also work through our example. I've been humbled by the kind words of so many. If a single person can find inspiration and be drawn closer to God because of my story, I feel blessed.

Someone told me that his dad had died from prostate cancer at an even younger age than me. Since childhood, he had been holding some resentment toward his father for leaving him at such a young age. By hearing what I was going through and understanding that his dad had probably experienced the same struggles and emotions, he was able to heal some of those wounds.

I don't fully understand how I can be the person setting the example. I know me too well. I watched my best friend become an inspiration to people after the death of his son. He is an amazing example of faith and joy-filled suffering. I don't understand how I can be inspiring too. Maybe I don't know myself as well as I think I do.

There is comfort in knowing that my faith must be real if others are seeing it in my example. It is easy to doubt and think that maybe I'm only going through the motions of my faith. To be told that others are seeing Jesus in me is an incredible feeling.

I have even heard people at work say that they are impressed by how I'm handling this journey. I have no idea if they have faith or not, and I haven't shared any of my story with them except to tell them I'm battling cancer. Somehow, they are seeing this Christian joy in me too. It can't be hidden.

You are the light of the world. A city set on a hill cannot be hid. Nor do men light a lamp and put it under a bushel, but on a stand, and it gives light to all in the house. Let your light so shine before men, that they may see your good works and give glory to your Father who is in heaven.
Matthew 5:14-16

We never know who is being helped by our example, or how it is helping them.

With such tremendous support and prayer, why didn't those prayers help me?

Why have I not been cured?

It can be tough to see exactly how God answers prayers. He may not have given me an immediate cure, but perhaps he kept the cancer from getting even worse.

Maybe others needed to be inspired by my story, and *they* were the ones helped by everyone's prayers.

Perhaps I needed more to offer up as redemptive suffering, and it is my friend who is being helped. The prayers could be giving me the strength to endure this fight.

Regardless of how God has answered these thousands of prayers people have offered for me, I know prayer works.

I continue to take this battle to God in my own prayer. Two experiences in particular stand out to me.

I've prayed many times as Jesus did—that this cup be taken from me. One night after a Lenten book study at church I decided to stop in the chapel to pray before going home. It was late. I was alone in the dim chapel.

The only sound I heard through the silence was the creaking of the building in the winter wind.

Once again, I prayed that God would take this from me. As I sat in silence, I heard God's answer very plainly in my mind.

"Don't run away from this cross. Jesus didn't run away from His."

A few weeks later I was kneeling after receiving communion at Mass. I gazed at the crucifix as I prayed. I had had a particularly difficult week, so I asked God *why* He wouldn't take this cross away from me.

Moments later He told me that He allowed me the *privilege* of having this cancer so that I could bear this cross for my friend. God told me that my friend needs me to continue to offer it up for him as redemptive suffering.

Prayer is not like a vending machine. We shouldn't think we can put a prayer in and expect the answer we want. But if we pray and trust in God, He often does give us answers—even if we'd prefer a different one.

One thing we need to keep in mind when we pray is that there is also the Enemy who wants to discourage us. Even when we pray and have faith, Satan attacks.

> *Finally, be strong in the Lord and in the*
> *strength of his might. Put on the whole*
> *armor of God, that you may be able to*
> *stand against the wiles of the devil.*
> Ephesians 6:10-11

As I was at the peak of chemotherapy and struggling with the side effects, I experienced an attack.

I was having a hard time sleeping, so I got up in the middle of the night to stretch my legs and try to reset. When I laid back down, every frustration and worry from this cancer hit.

All at once.

The reality of the permanent surgical side effects, the fatigue, the weight gain, the weakness, the long road ahead to lose weight and gain strength back, how my moodiness has certainly got to be offending my friends and driving them away, the hot flashes, a gut feeling that I'm not going to beat this, my worry about leaving my wife and kids behind, etc., etc., etc.

It was so strange, though. It was not a sequential series of thoughts and worries. I was not just thinking about it that night.

It ALL hit, ALL AT ONCE. It was some odd and uncomfortable infused knowledge. It just WAS.

It is hard to explain, but it had to be supernatural. And it had to be from the Enemy. God doesn't give us worry and frustration.

I said the St. Michael prayer, then lay in bed awake until morning.

St. Michael the Archangel, defend us in battle, be our protection against the wickedness and snares of the devil. May God rebuke him we humbly pray; and do thou, O Prince of the Heavenly host, by the power of God, cast into hell Satan and all the evil spirits who prowl about the world seeking the ruin of souls. Amen.

I got up in the morning disturbed by the experience, but solidly grateful to God. I know God is working in my and so many others' lives. If we pray, Satan can never take hold of us.

Reflection Questions

1. How do you respond when others see qualities in you that you don't see in yourself?

2. When someone compliments you, do you feel unworthy? Do you feel like you don't live up to how they see you? Is this humility, or something else?

3. In what ways might God be using your struggles or challenges to inspire those around you? How can you turn to God to understand His purpose for your life?

14

ONE STEP CLOSER

Now that chemo was done it was time to move to the next phase of treatment.

First, we needed to address a related issue. For many men, the incontinence side effect of surgery improves to nearly normal. After six months, my surgeon gave me the news that if it hadn't improved by now, it was not going to. The nearly five hour surgery was simply too damaging to the nerves. I needed to undergo another surgery to address the problem.

With another major surgery imminent, I texted the priest who had anointed me twice before and scheduled another anointing. Two years earlier I would not have envisioned ever receiving the Sacrament of Anointing, except perhaps in old age. I absolutely never thought about needing to receive it three times in two years. But each time I received it I felt the presence of God as He gave me the strength and comfort I needed to bear these crosses.

After a night in the hospital, I was back home. It was another frustration in this struggle, but I was happy that something could be done. A week after surgery we celebrated the high school graduation of one of our kids. It was a great way to take my mind off myself and focus on my family again.

Because the cancer was so aggressive, the doctors threw the book at it. They chose a trifecta of treatments. I had finished chemotherapy. Now that the second surgery was done it was time to move on to hormone deprivation therapy before radiation.

The formal name is "androgen deprivation therapy", or ADT for short.

ADT is the gold standard for prostate cancer treatment. For almost all men, it is the only treatment they receive.

I was already receiving a quarterly shot for this same purpose, which was begun with chemo. An additional drug in pill form would work with it to ensure not a single drop of testosterone remained in my body. I would be on this therapy for an additional eighteen months.

The side effects were numerous.

It didn't take long to start becoming moody. I treated the people closest to me the worst. I would snap at them for the littlest things. I would make unnecessary biting and snarky passive-aggressive comments. I would be sarcastic, but not in the usual fun, joking way that people have come to expect from me.

I hope I have apologized well enough to everyone I've hurt. I hope I did not cause permanent damage to any relationships. I hope they understand that they mean the world to me and I'm not being myself.

> *Put on then, as God's chosen ones, holy*
> *and beloved, compassion, kindness,*
> *lowliness, meekness, and patience,*
> *forbearing one another and, if one has a*
> *complaint against another, forgiving each*
> *other; as the Lord has forgiven you, so you*
> *also must forgive.*
> Colossians 3:12-13

I started to become weaker as muscle atrophy began. I could have stayed somewhat stronger if I had worked out more. But without testosterone, the motivation to exercise disappears too.

As is the case in most households, I'm called upon to open the stubborn jars in the kitchen. I realized how bad my weakness had become when I could no longer successfully help my wife with this. I had become weaker over time without noticing it. The first time I could no longer open a jar I was furious. It didn't help that becoming more emotional is a side effect too.

Luckily, my wife is very understanding and willingly took on more things around the house because of my weakness and fatigue.

To help with some of the side effects of both chemotherapy and ADT, a steroid is prescribed. If you have ever been on steroids, you know that it is hard to sleep while taking them. I rarely slept well, nor got a full night's rest.

I was perpetually exhausted. After work, I would sit on the couch until bedtime. If I knew I wanted to do something after work, I would make sure I slept in that morning.

My wife had a perfect analogy to help me understand what I needed to do. She said that my energy level each day is like a bowl full of spoons. I start the day with only so many of them, so I need to decide where I want to spend them before I take them out of the bowl.

I never would have thought about it like that, but she was right. My energy bank could only hold so much.

One of the worst side effects is hot flashes. Perhaps I'll gain no sympathy from women. But going between being cold and in a matter of seconds feeling like I've walked into a boiler room in July is no fun. And it happens ten or twenty times every day. I'm thankful my wife puts up with me constantly taking the bed covers on and off all night with each hot flash.

It was also time to talk about radiation. Unlike the other treatments, this one could conceivably be optional.

My wife and I met with the radiation oncologist who had been highly recommended by my surgeon. He said he had recommended him to his own family. Like all of the doctors I had worked with, we immediately liked him and came to trust in his judgment.

He was a younger doctor who was well-versed in the current state of radiation oncology. He also held a PhD, and we would later find out he had done some research with a friend of mine while they were both working on their doctorates. Having trust in your medical professionals during this makes it a lot easier.

Of all the treatments, this one concerned me the most because of the potential to cause other cancers, along with permanently damaging healthy cells and causing a myriad of health problems.

It did not take me long to do some math to put it in perspective. The treatment would expose me over eight weeks to the same amount of radiation as more than 700,000 chest X-rays.

As we discussed the details with the doctor, I joked that after twenty-five years it was nice that my quantum physics class in college was finally becoming useful! My wife was not amused. I remember her chiding me as we left the appointment, "I had more questions, but you and the doctor were nerding out about energy levels and linear accelerators!"

There were risks with radiation, but there was also a big risk without it. This cancer should not have hit me this young. It should not have grown so fast. It should not have been aggressive enough to spread so rapidly.

It quickly became obvious that even with many risks, it was the right thing to do.

We needed to wait a couple of months to start so that my body could recover from the chemotherapy before we attacked it with radiation.

Once radiation is started, it is five days per week for eight weeks. There is no taking breaks.

As I looked at the calendar, I realized that if I started radiation as soon as it was safe to do so, it would mean canceling a trip I had been planning for years.

My best friend and I had been talking for years about taking an epic trip together to celebrate our milestone birthdays. This was going to be the year we did it.

We planned to attend the National Championship Air Races. We had tickets bought and a hotel room reserved. Most importantly, we had permission from our wives to be gone for a week!

Would radiation mean we had to cancel a once-in-a-lifetime trip that we had been planning for years?

Aside from the fact that we had been looking forward to it for so long, I really needed this trip. I needed to take my mind off of everything for a while and have fun without worrying about the next appointment or next treatment.

I needed some normal.

I was relieved to hear the doctor say that he would be comfortable delaying radiation for up to six months to find a convenient time to do it. He believed that the hormone therapy would keep any remaining cancer under control well enough to give me that flexibility.

Another look at the calendar showed that I could start radiation the week I got back from the air races, and then finish two days before Thanksgiving—in time to take our usual family trip to visit my wife's family. Praise God for the little blessings.

My friend and I had the adventure we had been planning for so long, and yes, it took my mind off my health for a while. A lot of laughter, a lot of relaxation, a lot of airplanes, and sharing a few drinks together will do that.

A week-long epic trip was just the thing I needed.

We returned from our trip on a Monday. On Thursday I reported for my first radiation treatment.

At least radiation for prostate cancer is quick and painless, although there are some very unpleasant side effects during it. The staff did a good job of getting me in and out quickly. I would stop in on my way to work and was usually out in fifteen minutes.

It became part of my routine. At the same time, it was a real slog to keep up with radiation. Monday through Friday for eight weeks. A total of thirty-nine treatment sessions.

On the Tuesday before Thanksgiving, I had my last radiation treatment. My wife and oldest daughter accompanied me to that one.

It is traditional to ring a bell when radiation treatment is finished. While I sat in the waiting room for every one of those thirty-nine treatments, I would look at that bell and think for a moment about how nice it will be to ring it and mark one more step in this journey complete.

I hopped off the treatment table, thanked the staff, and came out to ring the bell. My wife, daughter, and I celebrated with brunch at one of our favorite spots on the way home.

Rejoice always, pray constantly, give
thanks in all circumstances; for this is the
will of God in Christ Jesus for you.
1 Thessalonians 5:16-18

Later that night, I was sitting on the couch resting when I heard the beeping of our front door code being entered. I looked up and there was my best friend holding a bottle of bourbon. Before he turned it around for me to see what brand it was, he explained that he had found the perfect bottle of bourbon to celebrate a cancer patient. I could tell from the grin on his face that it was going to be good.

Heaven's Door bourbon.

Luckily, we both share an identical sense of humor.

We drank way too much of that bottle that night. After he left, I reflected on the day. The treatment milestone. The morning with family. The evening with a close friend.

Thanksgiving was just two days away, and I couldn't ignore how much I had to be grateful for.

Reflection Questions

1. What role does patience play in your faith, especially when dealing with long and difficult challenges?

2. How do humor and friendship serve as a reminder of God's love and support in hard moments?

3. In what ways can you celebrate the milestones in a long, difficult journey with gratitude, knowing that every step is part of God's plan for you?

15

DECIDING TO LIVE

I had surgery behind me. I had chemotherapy behind me. I had radiation behind me.

I was on the home stretch. But that home stretch was a long one.

I would remain on hormone blockers for another thirteen months.

Another thirteen months of moodiness, weakness, fatigue, insomnia, weight gain, and hot flashes.

Another thirteen months of spending twenty minutes on Saturday mornings sorting pills for the following week. I take nineteen pills every day. With my pill organizer, I feel like an old man. But now I understand why the elderly need help making sure they take the right medications!

As silly as it sounds, I refused to be sick. I refused to believe I couldn't do everything I wanted to do. I pushed through. While that attitude helped me tolerate it, that is not a strategy that works very well.

I would often lie down in the middle of the day and wonder why I was so tired.

Oh yeah. I have stage 4 cancer.

Even my wife did not know how bad I felt. And I felt terrible. I tried to keep the worst days to myself. I especially kept them away from the kids. Throughout all of this, my kids showed a maturity and kindness far beyond their years, but they did not need to know the toll this was taking on me.

The Lord is near to the brokenhearted,
and saves the crushed in spirit.
Psalm 34:18

The appointments with the doctors were routine now. I was seeing my surgeon, my medical oncologist, and my radiation oncologist every three months.

Each time, my PSA level was tested to check that the cancer remained under control. And each time, it was undetectable.

Until one visit with my radiation oncologist when the PSA level came back from the lab slightly above undetectable.

I had completed chemotherapy and radiation. I was currently on androgen deprivation therapy. There was no reason the cancer should be breaking through that much treatment.

Unless the cancer was just that aggressive.

My oncologist thought that it was likely a lab error. I could tell he was slightly concerned, but he did not seem to be *too* worried. There was an appointment coming up in a couple of weeks with another of my doctors, so we decided to wait and see what the PSA was at that visit.

It was the same routine with this news as with all of the previous news. I told my wife, then my kids, then my family, then my two closest friends.

Word got out to more of my friends. Then the texts started coming in letting me know they were praying for me.

Praise God, when we retested my PSA level it was undetectable. It must have been a lab error just like the doctor thought. Talking with him about it, he told me that if my PSA actually had been coming up while on the androgen deprivation therapy, it would mean that the cancer had become resistant to treatment. I would have had about eighteen months to live.

With gratitude that it was a false alarm, I continued on the treatment plan.

Several months later I noticed that my left upper leg was numb. It felt like your face feels after novocaine at the dentist.

These cancer treatments all cause some strange symptoms. But it did seem odd to be a side effect. It had been a year since I finished chemo and six months since I finished radiation. Maybe it was a side effect of the hormone therapy. But I had been on the hormone therapy for a year and a half already. It did not seem like it would be a side effect from that either.

After about two weeks I decided to get it checked out. I didn't know which doctor to go to since I didn't know what the cause was. I decided to start with my primary care doctor. He suspected it to be a nerve issue, so he ordered a lumbar X-ray.

The radiology department is in the basement of the building, so less than thirty minutes later I was back in the exam room.

I waited for the doctor to return, realizing that I would not be done in time for my golf league. I looked out the window and saw a downpour start. Soon afterward I received a text that golf league was canceled. At least that problem was solved! Sometimes it's those little blessings that make life better.

The doctor knocked and came back in. The X-ray showed a growth on one of my lumbar vertebrae, which explained the numbness. The cause was no longer a mystery.

However, the radiologist noted that it could be metastasis of the cancer. My doctor scheduled an MRI to get a better look.

Unfortunately, insurance required pre-approval before the MRI. Because of the time they needed to process the paperwork, it would be ten days before we had more information about the growth on my spine.

Prostate cancer typically spreads to the lymph nodes first, like mine did. The next place it goes is the bones—usually the spine.

My doctors told me it would be unusual for the cancer to spread while on treatment. But I knew this cancer had been oddly aggressive and had not been following the rules. It did not seem out of the realm of possibility that it could be spreading.

It fit the pattern well. Why would I have these issues if it were not cancer? Especially since the spine is the next place it would go.

I was hopeful this was nothing, yet I also knew the reality that there was a strong possibility this was not good.

When I got home from the appointment, my wife and I talked about it and decided to approach it with the kids like we always did—with a gentle mention.

We didn't believe there was any reason to worry the kids. After all, we didn't know with certainty if this actually was bad news or if it was something completely unrelated to the cancer.

We simply told the kids that I had a test that showed there might be some more problems with the cancer and that I had a follow-up scheduled in ten days to take a closer look.

That night after the kids were in bed, my wife and I stood in the kitchen and talked privately. If this ended up being bad news like it seemed it could be, what would we do?

We talked about when I would quit work. Should I work as long as I can to maximize income before the life insurance payout?

Should I quit earlier so we could have as much time as possible together as a family?

We decided to meet in the middle of the two options. I would work until I could qualify for disability insurance payments.

After my wife went to bed that night, I stayed up and made sure my funeral plan was updated and that the financial information in my "death binder" was current.

For several years—even before I had cancer—I started keeping all the information my wife would need to know in the event of my death in a black binder in our desk. My funeral wishes. Life insurance policies. Passwords. Bank accounts. After my cancer diagnosis I added some heartfelt letters to my wife, the kids, and a couple of friends. In my light-hearted way, I labeled it, "I'm Dead. Now What?"

It was starting to seem all too real that it could be important now.

When I crawled into bed, I laid awake thinking about what kind of last big family trip to take. Probably to Sanibel Island, Florida where we've enjoyed going so often together.

It was about time for another guys' trip. Where should the last one be? Surely it should involve a brewery somewhere.

The next day, like always, I texted my two closest friends. When I first found out that the cancer had become aggressive, I asked my best friend to give the eulogy at my funeral should it come to that. At least that arrangement was taken care of!

Should I ask the bigger group for prayers? I could definitely use them again.

Not yet. There is a chance this is not more cancer. I don't want to start rumors.

My family and two of the finest prayer warriors among my friends were on it. That would be enough for now.

I tried to go about my routine while I waited for the MRI appointment. Except for some extra trips to the chapel to pray, I lived like I always do.

It was the longest ten days of my life.

At about this same time, my mom was admitted to the hospital with multiple systems failure, and it was not looking good. Visiting her each day unquestionably helped keep my mind off my own problems.

It also helped keep things in perspective for me.

Not only was she nearing the end of her life, but when I looked out of her hospital window, I could see Children's Hospital across the street. I can't look at that hospital now without being reminded of my friend and what he and his wife endured losing their son in that building. I was privileged to spend many hours with them and their son while they held vigil at his bedside.

Come to me, all who labor and are heavy laden, and I will give you rest. Take my yoke upon you, and learn from me; for I am gentle and lowly in heart, and you will find rest for your souls. For my yoke is easy, and my burden is light.
Matthew 11:28-30

Finally, the day of my MRI arrived. I showed up at the hospital that morning and was taken back to radiology immediately. I lay down on the table, and then the technician placed headphones on me to help block out the deafening sound of the MRI machine. When they asked what style of music I preferred to listen to during the scan, I chose Christian praise and worship music.

Then she wrapped me in a sheet, placed a cloth over my eyes, and began moving me into the MRI tube. As she did that the similarities to being wrapped up, placed in a coffin, and buried hit me.

I am not one to be bothered by medical procedures. I am not claustrophobic. I have had many MRIs and have never had a problem. This one was different. My heart was pounding. I felt like I was starting to hyperventilate. I have never had a panic attack, but I imagine they feel like I was beginning to feel.

I focused on my breathing and focused on the music. I prayed. And I calmed down. Twenty minutes later, I was done.

I walked to my car and drove to the funeral home to meet Dad and my sister. Mom had passed the day before.

That afternoon, I got a call from my doctor's nurse. The MRI showed spinal arthritis that is more advanced than would be expected for my age, likely worsened by the radiation and the hormone therapy. It also validated that nerve compression was causing my leg numbness.

The news that I was waiting for, though, was that it was not cancer!! The cancer had not spread!

Deo gratias!

Ever since I was diagnosed with cancer, my outlook on life changed a little more with each challenge. Ultimately, the busyness and routine of life would return. Although the cancer was life-changing, I did not change my life.

People have asked me what I would do differently if the cancer became terminal. The answer is—not much. Terminal illness does not become an excuse for indulgence, regardless of what our culture says.

The question inspired me to think about the proverbial "bucket list". I soon realized that that was not the right way to think about it. Instead, I made a list of the things I should be doing now to have a great life regardless of how long that life is. A "good life list" instead of a bucket list.

I would double down on what I am already doing. More time with family. More time with friends. More prayer. Maybe an extra family trip and another guys' trip.

With this latest scare, I was convinced more than ever that the cancer was going to kill me. Like from the beginning, there was no fear, only faith. The seriousness of this scare caused me to change my outlook more than any of my experiences with the cancer so far.

I decided it was time to start living like I wanted to live rather than as a cancer patient. I wanted to push myself out of my comfort zone. I am done acting like I have stage 4 cancer. I am done being sick.

And let us run with perseverance the race that is set before us, looking to Jesus the pioneer and perfecter of our faith.
Hebrews 12:1-2

Several friends, and one in particular, had been trying for over a year to get me to do a bootcamp-style workout with them. I had all the excuses. I am not in good enough shape to exercise that way. It's outdoors year-round regardless of the weather. Most of all, it is at 5:15 am. That is where they lost me. I don't get up that early.

When one of them made the offer again shortly after this latest concern that the cancer had spread, I remembered that I wanted to start going outside my comfort zone and start living. After more than a year of "no" every time he asked, that day he about fell over when I said "yes".

I told my wife. She said I'd never keep up with them.

I told my best friend. He smiled and laughed.

As the two people who know me better than anyone else, I understood their reaction. It did not sound like me. But now I had something to prove. I was determined to prove them wrong.

Someone believed in me and my ability and determination to do this. He thought I could do it. I was determined to prove him right.

After I started to work out, my fatigue understandably got a lot worse. I was sleeping even more than before. I was constantly sore. It turns out that pretending you don't have stage 4 cancer doesn't work that well. But I enjoyed working out with these guys and my mental health was dramatically improving. Altogether, I felt better.

One of my doctors told me, "You shouldn't be doing this well after everything we've done to you."

That is an interesting way to put it. "Everything we've done to you." As if I am the victim of something.

I think he meant it somewhere between an observation and a compliment.

There were many times I would think that this isn't as bad as everyone (including myself) is making it out to be. I may be exhausted and not feel very well, but I'm still going to work like normal and doing a lot of what I like to do.

Then I realize that I've had pretty much every possible cancer treatment—surgery, chemotherapy, radiation, and ADT. I may not be bedridden, but this is serious.

Maybe I have not given myself enough grace to be tired and weak. Maybe I should have given in more.

But that is not my personality. I refuse to be sick.

Reflection Questions

1. In what ways do you see God working in your life even when circumstances seem overwhelming?

2. Have you ever had a moment where you had to accept a reality that was different than what you had hoped for? How did you find peace in that?

3. How can you "push through" difficult circumstances while also giving yourself the grace to heal and rest—physically, emotionally, and spiritually?

16

FAITH IN THE WAITING

A friend asked me a question when I was about halfway through treatment.

"How will this all end?"

I looked at him and said, "Hopefully not in my death!"

I knew what he meant. The fact is, the treatment ends with a whimper, not a bang. There is no final test to say that I am cancer free. There is no final treatment appointment.

The treatment ends the morning I take the last pills. Then, my body starts a slow recovery. My doctor tells me that I will not even start to feel better for nine months to a year after finishing treatment.

Yes, the cancer is treated. But the reality is that this is not a cancer that typically gets cured. It is usually merely slowed down and will eventually return. When I asked my oncologist about it, he said that we were much more intense with treatment than in a typical case. There is a chance we actually did cure it.

How will we know?

He said that if I live another ten years without it coming back, then we know we cured it.

Pretty simple and low-tech.

After taking the last pills, we monitor the PSA level every three months for two years. Then every six months for another three years. Then annually for five more years. At that point, we can call it cured.

Ten years of waiting for the phone call with the test results. Each time wondering when I answer the phone if this is the call where the doctor says everything is fine. Or the one where he says the cancer is back.

At each appointment with the doctor—is it the one where the doctor and I spend our appointment time catching up like old friends, or the one where we talk about the next steps for treatment?

At least if it comes back there will inevitably have been some medical advances in the meantime.

Even after I am done with treatment there is plenty to offer up. I do it willingly. God can do amazing things with our suffering.

> *If one member suffers, all suffer together;*
> *if one member is honored, all rejoice*
> *together.*
> 1 Corinthians 12:26

There remains a long road ahead to recovery. I will never be the same as I was physically, emotionally, or spiritually. But I'm trying to surrender to God's will more completely each day.

I have read a lot about cancer. Among many other things, I've read that the transition from cancer patient to cancer survivor can be an emotional one.

It's true.

It has been my identity for three years—*Cancer Patient.* In a way, it has been a source of self-worth. People expressed their care, concern, and love because of it. Now as I finish treatment, they don't. Do they still care about me?

What's my new identity if it's no longer "cancer patient"?

I'm not sure how to go back to the person I was.

Maybe that's what God has in mind. To no longer be the person that I was.

But who am I now?

"Cancer survivor" doesn't seem to be the complete description of the new me.

And I am sure that he who began a good
work in you will bring it to completion at
the day of Jesus Christ.

Philippians 1:6

Before it happened, I could not have predicted that I'd be on this journey. And I cannot predict the next part of it either.

While it hasn't been easy, I'm proud of how far I've come and I'm eternally grateful.

Grateful that I survived.

Grateful for my wife and kids, my family, and their prayers and support.

Grateful for my closest friends who were there for me and were my strongest prayer warriors.

Grateful for the community that stepped up, expressed their concern, and prayed for me.

Grateful for the opportunity and privilege God gave me to use my suffering to help my best friend get through his own suffering.

Grateful to God that I could always see His awesome hand in this.

And grateful to God for His loving care throughout all of it.

I have fought the good fight, I have
finished the race, I have kept the faith.
2 Timothy 4:7

Reflection Questions

1. How can waiting become a time of spiritual growth rather than frustration? What practices or disciplines help you remain faithful during these times?

2. When you reflect on God's presence, how have you experienced His love and peace in ways that you didn't expect?

3. How can you help others carry their crosses, even if you're carrying one of your own?

ABOUT THE AUTHOR

A devoted husband, father of four, and steadfast friend, Jeff's life revolves around faith, family, and community.

As a faithful and active Catholic, Jeff finds joy and purpose in his involvement with church activities, striving to live out his faith in every aspect of his life.

A cancer patient and survivor, Jeff draws strength from his faith and relationships, using his journey to inspire and lift up others.

This book is born from his love of storytelling and his passion for sharing the hope and resilience his faith has given him.

Jeff holds a chemical engineering degree along with an MBA and works as an engineering manager for a major company.

When not working, he enjoys flying as a licensed commercial pilot and spending time with his loved ones. Living in the Midwest, he is endlessly curious and would pursue a million hobbies if time allowed, but his greatest joy is found in his faith and in being a husband, father, and friend.

To inquire about having Jeff speak at your church or business event, please contact him at four.saints.publishing@gmail.com.

Jeff can speak about his cancer journey, as well as many other faith and business topics.

Jeff is also available for parish retreats and missions.

www.ingramcontent.com/pod-product-compliance
Lightning Source LLC
Chambersburg PA
CBHW021110130626
46554CB00002B/619

* 9 7 9 8 9 9 2 2 1 2 8 0 8 *